How to ...

get the most from your

COLES NOTES

Key Point

Basic concepts in point form.

Close Up

Additional hints, notes, tips or background information.

Watch Out!

Areas where problems frequently occur.

Quick Tip

Concise ideas to help you learn what you need to know.

Remember This!

Essential material for mastery of the topic.

COLES NOTES

Your Guide to ...

Investing in Stocks

Designing a portfolio

How to research & evaluate stocks

Taxes & capital gains

———————— ABOUT COLES NOTES ————————

COLES NOTES have been an indispensable aid to students on five continents since 1948.

COLES NOTES now offer titles on a wide range of general interest topics as well as traditional academic subject areas and individual literary works. All COLES NOTES are written by experts in their fields and reviewed for accuracy by independent authorities and the Coles Editorial Board.

COLES NOTES provide clear, concise explanations of their subject areas. Proper use of COLES NOTES will result in a broader understanding of the topic being studied. For academic subjects, Coles Notes are an invaluable aid for study, review and exam preparation. For literary works, COLES NOTES provide interesting interpretations and evaluations which supplement the text but are not intended as a substitute for reading the text itself. Use of the NOTES will serve not only to clarify the material being studied, but should enhance the reader's enjoyment of the topic.

© Copyright 1998 and Published by
COLES PUBLISHING. A division of Prospero Books
Toronto – Canada
Printed in Canada

Cataloguing in Publication Data

Your guide to—investing in stocks :
designing a portfolio ; how to research & evaluate stocks ; taxes & capital gains

(Coles notes) Includes bibliographical references.
ISBN 0-7740-0604-8

1. Stocks. I. Series.

HG4661.Y68 1999   332.63'.22   C99-930727-4

Publisher: Nigel Berrisford
Editing: Paul Kropp Communications
Book design: Karen Petherick, Markham, Ontario
Layout: Richard Hunt

Manufactured by Webcom Limited
Cover finish: Webcom's Exclusive DURACOAT

Contents

CHAPTER ONE

The basics of investing in stocks

The ups and downs of the stock market can create both excitement and concern for an investor. Historical performance has shown that stocks, over the long term, have outperformed every other asset class, including real estate and fixed-income investments. But there are periods in the Canadian economic cycle or in the global economy when even the most experienced investors will face uncertainty and have their patience tested. These times may also provide astute investors with cash, the opportunity to buy when the market and the stocks they are interested in are down in value. This is precisely the time when it is difficult to find the courage to buy.

To keep it all in perspective, remember the words of Mark Twain: "There are two times in a man's life when he should not speculate: When he can't afford it, and when he can."

This book focuses on investing in stocks. This is not to suggest than your portfolio will or should be 100 percent equities. After all, stocks investments do not guarantee your capital. For a primer on investing in bonds, stocks and mutual funds, see Coles Notes' *Your Guide to Basic Investing*. This book introduces investment concepts and builds upon them. For more information about mutual funds, see Coles Notes' *Your Guide to Mutual Funds*. The book in your hands concentrates on the more sophisticated investing involved with buying and selling stocks.

There are many ways to invest in stocks:

- **direct purchases** through a stock broker or discount broker
- **equity or balanced** mutual funds, which provide a convenient, professionally managed portfolio
- **company pension plans** managed by a pension plan manager as part of a benefit package through an employer.

Regardless of how you choose to invest, it is important to understand how the equity markets work and how investment decisions are made.

Investing in stocks can be risky. Ask anyone who started investing in 1998. For years prior, it seemed that almost anyone could invest in blue chip stocks and make money. Then, starting in April 1998, even the "safest" blue chip stocks started to fall in value. September 1998 ended the worst three-month period in 16 years as Canada and much of the world faced the worst market period since the Depression of the 1930s.

When comparing performance numbers, you will see differences between the calendar-year performance and your total return over your personal holding period. Suppose you invested $1,000 in the TSE300 index in December 1983. By the end of December 1998, your portfolio would have been worth $3,930, up over 293 percent. Comparatively, if you have put $1,000 in 91-day treasury bills, over the same period, your portfolio would have been worth $3,233, up over 223 percent. (Interest rates fell over this 15-year period. The treasury bills earned an average of 11.6 percent in 1984 and only 4.7 percent in 1998. The returns ranged from 32.5 percent in one calendar year to –14.8 percent, with five years showing negative returns.)

That said, you can be a successful investor, as long as you understand what makes the stock market work, don't risk more than you are prepared to lose and are patient. But anyone who believes picking winning stocks is the key to financial success is forgetting two things: one, the impact tax has on net worth and two, how critical regular saving is to building true wealth.

Over the long term, investors earn more than those who rely on fixed income investments. But the psychological necessity of being patient, or buying a good stock when it is down in value, is sometimes more easily recognized than done. Many investors believe that the baby boomers will become dedicated savers and investors and their dollars will help push up the value of the stock markets.

Canadians often look at investing in Canada rather than investing in other countries. Certainly, Canadians have better access to information about local companies whose businesses they understand. But in the late 1990s, the Asian contagion and the Latin American Crisis rudely reminded investors that what happens in other parts of the world can affect what happens at home.

BALANCING YOUR INVESTMENTS

Just as you should not keep all your money in a single financial vehicle, neither should you have all your money in stocks. Building an investment portfolio requires you not only to select investments appropriate for your goals, but to define your investment goals and objectives and then manage those investments.

Diversification, sometimes called strategic asset allocation, is used to reduce some of the risk in investing. Different investments respond differently to economic changes. If an investor can select investments that do not all respond in the same way to these changes, it is possible to reduce, although not totally eliminate, some investment risk.

The "right" asset mix for you will depend on your investment objectives, your investment experience, the economic outlook, the number of years your money will be invested and your tolerance for risk. It has been said that Canadians like safe investments and have shied away from some investments because they were risky. Sometimes you might consider an investment to be risky because you don't really understand how it works. It is only when you understand how an investment works and what makes it tick that you can determine whether or not it meets your objectives.

Your portfolio will not just contain stocks. You will also hold some cash, have bank accounts and may even have some Guaranteed Investment Certificates (GICs) or bonds. The amount you have in cash or cash-like investments depends on how much you need to have available for day-to-day needs, or how much you have waiting for the ideal buying opportunity to add some more stocks to your portfolio. The percentage you hold in income-earning investments, or investments that have guarantees, depends on your investment experience, your risk tolerance and the outlook you have for the stock market.

THE STOCK MARKET

The stock market and the capital markets are regulated ways for buyers and sellers of financial products (stocks, bonds and other capital instruments) to come together. For many years, it was not unlike a farmers' market, where buyers and sellers came together to trade their wares. There is someone who wants to sell an investment and someone else who wants to buy it and only time will tell which one is getting the best deal.

Buyers can be individuals investing their RRSPs or other savings, or institutional investors, such as a corporation or a pension plan. The price an investor is willing to pay for a stock is based on what the buyer and the seller believe the stock is worth. Today, much of the buying and selling is done electronically and anonymously. Of course, the stock market is more highly regulated than a farmers' market. To make a trade, you have to call your broker to place an order to buy or sell a stock. Your broker will then place an order that will be processed electronically with someone interested in selling that stock to you or buying that stock from you.

Who are the key people involved in the buying and selling of securities?

The individual investor is interested in investing for growth or income.

The institutional investor manages money on behalf of corporations or on behalf of hundreds of individuals, such as a mutual fund manager or a pension fund manager.

A broker is the intermediary between investors and issuers, buyers and sellers, who want to buy and sell individual securities or raise money for various projects through new issues of securities.

A corporate issuer is a company looking to raise money for major projects or to finance debt in the capital markets through an initial public offering (IPO). A company must be prepared to go "public" with its financial statements and disclose all the facts of its operation so investors can make an informed decision as to whether or not to make an investment in the shares or debt of the corporation.

STOCKS MEAN OWNERSHIP

Stocks represent ownership in a corporation. Common shareholders are allowed to vote on all major decisions of the corporation and, theoretically, profit if a company does well (preferred shareholders have no voting rights). Shareholders have certain rights as owners of the corporation. Their rights include:

- electing the company's board of directors
- appointing independent auditors
- selling or merging the company
- voting on other key issues

Shareholders may also be paid dividends, which represent a share of the earnings of the company.

For each share owned, an investor is entitled to one vote. An investor who owns 20 percent of the stock holds 20 percent of the votes. Voting usually occurs at the annual general meeting, or at a special meeting. A shareholder who cannot attend the meeting can vote by **proxy**.

Loaners – people who hold bonds or corporate debt – are not investors. Loaners prefer to lend money in exchange for a favorable interest return on the loan and loaners also expect to have the principal amount repaid in the future.

FACTORS THAT AFFECT STOCK PRICES

Let's look at some of the factors that affect the price of a stock. Some factors will increase the price; others will cause the price to fall. These include:

- **supply and demand** for stocks. For example, if the boomers are saving for their retirement and their savings go overwhelmingly into the stock market, the demand for stocks would be expected to affect the overall price for shares.
- **investor expectations** for higher (or lower) stock prices. When prices start to fall, investors may decide to sell their investments, which can lower the price of any stock.
- **changing tax laws** that could make it easier, or more difficult, for a company to conduct its business. Other tax changes might increase or decrease the income consumers have available to purchase the goods or services manufactured by the company.
- **history of dividend payments**. Increasing dividends and/or expectation of corporate profits may positively affect the price of a stock.
- **reports of corporate earnings**, good and bad.
- **rumors**, even if they are false, can affect the price. In 1998, the chief financial officer of Northern Telecom commented that the company would not do as well as expected and this was enough to cause the stock to drop 20 percent.
- **economic news**. Employment figures, inflation data, construction starts, bankruptcies – all have an impact on the environment in which companies operate and their ability to be profitable.

- **political uncertainty**, such as when the President of the United States faces impeachment proceedings or a province wants to separate from the rest of Canada.
- **interest rates**. Rising interest rates may encourage people to move their money from the stock market into secure interest bearing investments, reducing the demand for stocks.

History indicates that there are other factors at play that affect stock prices. Although they do not apply all the time, some investors pay attention to:

- **the October effect**. Security prices tend to fall in October.
- **the Monday effect**. If there is bad news in the marketplace, prices tend to dip on Mondays, presumably because investors have been reading bad news in the papers over the weekend and act on Mondays.

Investing in one stock is always risky. The risk of a portfolio decreases as the number of stocks and the number of sectors the investor participates in increases. The stock market contains two types of risk: systematic risk and non-systematic risk. Systematic risk is the risk of the market itself, such as a bear market. Non-systematic risk is unique to the stock of a particular company, affected by such factors as poor management or the demand for that company's services. Investing in the stocks of three banks does not decrease systematic risk, and some would agree that it doesn't do much to reduce non-systematic risk if all the banks "look the same."

TYPES OF RISK

Investment in stocks is affected by stock market trends, economic conditions and company activities. There are different types of risks that investors have to evaluate and protect themselves from, as much as possible. The basic risks that can reduce the value of a portfolio are: business risk, market risk, liquidity risk and currency risk. The risk of interest rate changes, inflation and tax changes will also affect the portfolio's value.

- **Business risk** is related to running a business. Stock investors are investing in corporations. Some companies have good levels of sales, expanding market opportunities at home or globally, good financial statements, a committed labor force and strong management. Others don't.
- **Market risk** is related to the laws of supply and demand in the stock market. The laws of supply and demand simply stated are:

> The higher the demand for a good or service, the higher the price and conversely, the lower the demand, the lower the price.

Think of the housing market in Metropolitan Toronto in the late '80s or Vancouver in the late '90s. Interest rates were low and many people were interested in buying – the price of housing went up. Then the economy got soft and more people were interested in selling than buying – housing prices fell.

When people want to buy the stock of a particular company, this helps to push the price up. If few people want to buy the stock of a particular company, and many people want to sell their investment, the motivated sellers will have to reduce their asking price to make it more attractive to those buyers.

- **Liquidity risk** relates to the ability to turn the investment into cash quickly at a reasonable price. Some investments, like antiques, coins and artwork, cannot be turned into cash quickly. Other investments have so few potential buyers that sellers might have to sell their investments at a loss if they need their cash out.
- **The risk of losing purchasing power**. Inflation exists when there is a rise in the general level of prices and you need more income each year to maintain the same standard of living. Suppose you need $30,000 of income today. If inflation is increasing the cost of living at 2.5 percent per year (not much,

you might think), in 10 years you would require an annual income of about $38,400.

INVESTMENT STRATEGIES

Much of the investment research and the reports in the media focus on short-term results. What happened in the markets today, yesterday, last month? What might happen tomorrow? How you respond to short-term problems and opportunities relates to your investment strategy. The two most common are:

- **market timing**, which involves a certain amount of guess-work. You have to forecast the stock price of a particular company or the direction of the business cycle. As a long-term investment strategy, market timing is unreliable and few people can do it consistently, although "being in the right place at the right time" is always emotionally appealing. Many investors end up buying stock on old news, and selling before it hits the top. It's a disciplined investor who can buy when the stock market is near the bottom since we never know exactly where the bottom is until after the market has hit it and moved on.

- **buy and hold**. Another school of thought says investing is a long-term endeavor. These investors look at selecting good businesses to own and buy these stocks with the intention of holding them in their portfolio until the outlook for those companies change. During a bear market, buy-and-hold investors have to believe enough in this strategy to hold onto their shares when everyone around them is selling. It is also believed that excessive trading in a portfolio outside an RRSP generates a higher tax bill because taxes must be paid when profits are realized. The buy-and-hold strategy defers the taxes on growth and allows the pretax market value of the port-folio to accumulate.

There will be times when it will be profitable to act like a market timer and others when it will be profitable to buy and hold. But no one knows exactly when to do which.

Being a successful stock investor is not just about picking stocks; it is also about building an investment portfolio and involves defining your objectives, selecting investments appropriate to your goals, managing the investments in your portfolio and minimizing the tax payable.

CHAPTER TWO

What kind of investor are you?

INVESTOR OBJECTIVES AND GOALS

Before you build the portfolio that is right for you, you need to define your objectives. Of course, these objectives will change over time, depending on your employment status, financial responsibilities and the size of your net worth, so a regular review is also important.

Four factors are used to help define your objectives as an investor: your need for growth, income, safety and liquidity. For example, a highly employable computer analyst in her early 40s looking to retire early might be looking for growth with some safety and require no liquidity from her long-term retirement portfolio. A retired couple may be looking more for income and safety from their capital to supplement a modest pension. Stock investors are generally focused on growth and expect to be rewarded over time for taking the risk of investing in the stock market. The more growth an investor requires (or wants) from a portfolio, the riskier that portfolio will be.

The objectives of a portfolio must be integrated with your life goals and your current situation.

For example, if you are new to investing, you may be a more cautious investor than someone who has been investing all their adult life. Certainly, as you become more comfortable with investing and picking stocks, you may find yourself adding more risk to your portfolio. On the other hand, if you need to take income from your portfolio, you will want to have more in cash-type investments than you did during your saving years to be sure you don't have to sell any investments when they might be down in value.

11

No one should have money in the stock market that they are saving for a specific purpose in the next two to three years. Stock investments do not guarantee your principal – there is no guarantee that you will get back the money you invested.

RISK

Your risk level, or personal risk tolerance, is a measure of how comfortable you feel about the chance of losing any money in the markets over the short term. The greater your nervousness about fluctuations in the value of your portfolio, the lower your risk tolerance.

Studies of returns on investments over the past 40 years have shown a strong relationship between risk and reward, but investments with higher risks do *not* guarantee higher returns. Even good investments can have high risk and low returns over shorter periods of time. And some investments are just not good investments.

Most informed Canadians invest because they are willing to trade between the opportunity for higher long-term returns for the added investment risk. If you are not comfortable with the fact that there will be periods when the value of your investments will be down, even if it is only temporary, you may think of yourself as a saver rather than an investor.

Before you start investing, you need to consider the rates of return you could reasonably expect to make in the stock markets. Occasionally an investor will hit the jackpot, but the key to successful investing is discipline and savings. Even though annual returns throughout much of the 1990s were double-digit, sometimes over 20 percent or more a year for some investments, the long-term historical returns in the Canadian stock market are under 10 percent even when we add in the returns from reinvested dividends. Investors looking for double-digit returns year after year will be disappointed and may end up taking their money out of the stock market when it is at its lowest value.

Successful investors look at purchasing the shares of the best businesses. They take the emotion out of investing by doing thorough research and applying discipline to their purchases and sales. Select the asset classes you want to include in your portfolio and then within each asset class, pick the investments that you are comfortable with.

Some investors look at other successful investors to see what they have done. Some of the most successful long-term investors of all time include Warren Buffet, Sir John Templeton and Peter Lynch. These investors have a disciplined approach to picking stocks and have taken a long-term view of the companies they purchase. Lynch and Buffet agree that if you don't understand what the company does, you shouldn't be investing in it. For example, Buffet admits he stays away from technology stocks.

Some of their most famous quotes offer keys to successful investing:

"Most people get interested in stocks when everyone else is. The time to get interested is when no one else is. You can't buy what is popular and do well."

- Warren Buffet

"There is no such thing as a conservative stock."

- Peter Lynch

"The best time to invest is when you have the money."

- Sir John Templeton

GROWTH VERSUS VALUE

Two different investing styles are growth and value investing, although the difference between a **growth stock** and a **value stock** is sometimes subtle. *Securities Analysis,* by Benjamin Graham and David Dodd, was first published in 1934 and is still available today. This book outlines the fundamentals of value investing and some investors only apply the value orientation when picking their investments.

Most **growth** investors look first for rapid sales growth and are willing to pay for the anticipated future earnings. They would be willing to pay more, or a premium, for a stock than would a value investor because they believe the company will have rising corporate earnings that will ultimately push the value of the stock up.

Most **value** investors analyze the particular strength of a company, including the long-term financial strength and growth potential. These investors are looking for companies with share prices that appear to be undervalued, or relatively cheap in relation to the value of the company. Sometimes this investment style is referred to as "value investing." Value investors look for a relationship between the share price and the book value of the assets of the company (price to book) and want to buy the company when the shares are undervalued. Focusing on the selection of companies to invest in and not overpaying for the stock adds a margin of safety for the long-term investor. This method may not provide much excitement, but may reward the patient investor.

Different investment strategies seem to give better returns during different phases of the business cycle. For investors who do not believe in market timing, holding both value and growth stocks can build a better long-term portfolio.

ASSET ALLOCATION

Diversification or strategic asset allocation is used to reduce some of the risk in investing. Different investments respond differently to economic changes. For example, if an investor can select investments in asset classes that do not all respond in the same way to these changes, it is possible to reduce, although not totally eliminate, some investment risk.

Think of the familiar saying: "Don't put all your eggs in one basket!"

Diversification among asset classes does not eliminate the risk of poor returns – but it does apply a discipline to the selection of assets in an investment portfolio that can reduce the overall investment risk. Asset classes include cash, fixed-income investments, Canadian and international stocks, real estate and tangible investments.

There is no one "perfect" mix. The key is to balance risk and reward when building a portfolio. Some combinations of asset groups can reduce the investment risk in your portfolio. Your actual mix will depend on your risk tolerance, current market conditions and projections of future economic conditions.

A **conservative** asset mix designed for income might look like this:

	Percentage
Cash	10
Canadian fixed income	65
Canadian stocks	10
International stocks	5
Real estate and other tangibles	10
Total	100

This portfolio is weighted in favor of investments that are designed to create regular income. The Canadian equity investments in this conservative portfolio might be those paying regular dividend income, such as dividend stocks or dividend mutual funds.

An **aggressive** asset mix designed for long-term capital growth might look like:

	Percentage
Cash	5
Canadian fixed income	15
Canadian equity	35
International equity	35
Real estate and other tangibles	10
Total	100

This portfolio is weighted more heavily in assets designed for growth: Canadian and international equities, with investments in the other asset groups for additional diversification.

 One rule of thumb suggests the asset mix for an individual can be determined based on the person's age, using a percentage in fixed income investments equal to his or her age.

For example, someone who is 50 years of age might have 50 percent of a long-term portfolio in fixed-income investments. Someone who is 40 years old might have 40 percent of a portfolio in fixed-income investments, and so on.

Investors should also consider the size of their portfolio and the amount of cash needed each year to achieve personal goals. Someone who is retiring in 15 years and is just starting to focus on building a retirement nest egg might want to save more each year, or build a more aggressive portfolio to make up for lost time.

The "right" asset mix for you will depend on your investment objectives, your investment experience, the economic outlook, the number of years your money will be invested and your tolerance for risk. Sometimes you might consider an investment to be a risky because you don't really understand how it works. Once you understand what makes it tick, you can determine whether or not it meets your objectives.

TEST YOURSELF

You need to determine what kind of an investor you are. You might be a cautious, a moderate or an aggressive investor. Almost every financial institution has a risk-profile questionnaire designed to quiz you on your investment time frame, goals, experience and how you expect you will respond to risk. These questionnaires are based on research. Normally you complete one, add up the numbers that correspond to your answers, and voilà, you will find out what kind of an investor you are, according to the questionnaire. This in turn will help you develop the asset allocation that is right for your investment personality.

Each risk profile will ask you questions to try and determine your

- time horizon, when you need the money from your portfolio
- personal situation, including your age and the size of your portfolio
- your financial objectives
- your investment experience
- your attitude toward investment risk

Here's a sampling of the some of the questions you might be asked on one of these questionnaires. (Note: This is only a sampling of questions, **not** a scientifically designed questionnaire.)

Financial objectives

Your main investment objective for this money is:

( )   security and preserving capital

( )   creating regular income

( )   growth with some safety

( )   long-term growth to meet my future income needs

Time horizon

I will need to withdraw some money from my portfolio

( )   in less than 3 years

( )   in 3 to 5 years

( )   more than 5 but less than 10 years

( )   more than 10 years

How much of this portfolio might you need for personal or family emergencies?

( )   hard to say

( )   no more than 10 percent of it

( )   less than 5 percent of it

( )   none

Key personal information

The value of my investments is:

( )   less than $10,000

( ) $10,000–$25,000

( ) $25,001–$50,000

( ) $50,001–$100,000

( ) $100,001–$200,000

( )   over $200,000

My age is:

( )   under 25

( )   25–35

( )   36–50

( )   51–60

( )   61–70

( )   over 70

My income (not including income from my investments) is:
- ( ) less than $25,000
- ( ) $25,001–$50,000
- ( ) $50,001–$75,000
- ( ) $75,001–$150,000
- ( ) over $150,000

Investment experience

I have been an investor for
- ( ) over 10 years and have seen the ups and downs
- ( ) for 5 years and the markets have been good to me
- ( ) I'm just getting started

Risk tolerance

I know markets go up and down. When they go down, I can stay invested:
- ( ) for the long-term without worrying about selling out
- ( ) until I just can't take it any more
- ( ) for only a few months and then I'd move to something safer until the market starts to go up again

You are given the chance to buy into a new business for $10,000. You have a 50 percent change of getting back $50,000 within five years and a 50 percent chance of losing up to 50 percent of your original investment. Would you pay $10,000 to buy into the business?
- ( ) Yes, no question
- ( ) Maybe
- ( ) No, it's not for me

You'll then be asked to total up your score and be rated on one of a number of scales. Here are two sample scales:

Sample 1

	Percentage in Equities
Conservative growth and income	less than 40
Balanced growth and income	40–55
Long-term growth	55–65
Maximum long-term growth	more than 65

Sample 2

Security oriented	10
Balanced	40
Growth oriented	60

Each questionnaire will have its own scale. If you completed the questionnaires of two different financial institutions, you should find that they indicate a similar percentage in income and growth investments for your portfolio.

Don't forget to use your common sense here because evaluating risk tolerance and designing a portfolio are not academic exercises. Both are very personal. You'll also have to adjust your risk tolerance portfolio with the rate of return you need from your investment to achieve your investment goals. If your questionnaire describes you as a conservative investor, but the returns you might earn from a conservative portfolio are not enough for you to retire when you want to, you may have to be prepared to save more, retire later or move from a conservative portfolio to a more aggressive one to increase the returns your portfolio might be able to achieve. You should complete a new questionnaire every two or three years and whenever your time frame, personal situation, objectives and tolerance to risk seems to be changing. It is never a good idea to have a portfolio that is more aggressive than you are comfortable with.

Strategic asset allocation looks at the amount of risk investors are willing to have in their portfolio and selects an asset mix of stocks, bonds and cash to build a portfolio of different investments to minimize the downside risk in the portfolio and maximize the return potential for the desired level of risk. **Tactical asset allocation** looks at the investments in stocks, bonds and cash to maximize the return given changing market conditions by timing the market.

Although history shows that over the long term stock investments outperform bonds or cash, there are periods when bonds and cash outperform stocks. Most investors will want to include some bonds for stability and have some cash available for those opportune times to buy, when investors have reached the maximum point of pessimism in a bear market, just before the next bull run begins.

INSIDER TRADING

The securities regulators define an "insider" as someone who has inside knowledge about a company that has not yet been disclosed to the general public (including key executives, directors, those who hold more than 10 percent of the company's stock and others). These individuals have restrictions on the times they may trade their shares of the company and must file an insider trading report. They are not allowed to profit from their position at the public's expense.

You may have a friend or a broker who calls you with a **hot** tip that you "just can't miss with." It is illegal to make a trade based on insider information that has not been disclosed to the general public. Besides, there is no such thing as a "sure thing." You need to know what you are buying.

PROFESSIONAL TRADER

A professional trader is someone who makes a living trading on behalf of investors, such as a mutual fund money manager, or someone whose occupation is trading his or her own personal portfolio. A professional trader may have to report profits as regular income and lose the opportunity to handle profits as capital gains with the usual preferred tax treatment (where only 75 percent of profits on investments are taxed).

GAMBLER

For most people, assessing stocks varies from a hobby to an obsession. For some, investing takes on an air of gambling – and close beside the gambler is the speculator. Society has always had those individuals who are prepared to risk it all for the "big payoff" or those who fall prey to penny stock offerings or hot tips. If it was that easy, there would be a lot more millionaires around.

You need to determine if you are looking for solid, steady growth on your capital or if you are prepared to take a flier in the hopes that it will pay off big-time. But don't ever put your serious savings on a flier. You've just worked too hard for that. However, if something comes along that just sounds too good to let pass by, limit the amount you are prepared to invest to no more than 5–10 percent of your hard-earned savings.

CHAPTER THREE

Selecting stocks

There are a number of ways to decide on stocks that may be candidates for your portfolio. Most successful investors suggest you have to have a disciplined approach to selecting your stocks. If you get caught up in emotion or the hype of the moment, you are doomed to fail. Investors can:

- study the economy in which businesses operate
- invest only in certain types of stocks
- invest in only certain types of industries
- use fundamental analysis to study companies
- use technical analysis – charts or other techniques – to crunch the numbers to see how the stock market and other investors are evaluating a particular company

Successful investors are patient and research both the forest (the economy) and the trees (individual companies). They are looking for reasons to eliminate companies from their buy list, as well as for a few choice companies they can grow with over the long term.

No one method to assess the future price of a stock is foolproof. In fact, even if you use all the methods available to assess a stock, there are no guarantees you will always pick winners. But if you're careful, you can avoid loading up your portfolio with losers.

ECONOMIC CYCLE

The outlook for the Canadian economy sets the stage for Canadian businesses. By considering the overall economic conditions and outlooks for various types of business, investors look for the types of industries and companies with growth potential. For example, some stocks historically have been more sensitive to changes in interest rates than others. In the past, companies in the banking and utility sectors have benefited when interest rates fell. When interest rates appear to be rising, companies in the resource and manufacturing sectors have tended to benefit.

The economies of countries of the world go through business cycles, or periods of ups and down in economic activity.

PHASES OF A BUSINESS CYCLE

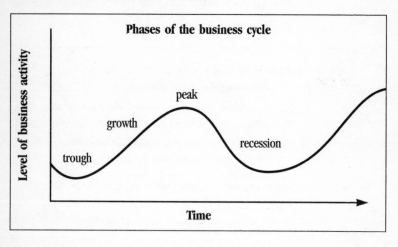

Different indicators are used to help assess the state of the economy:

- **Lagging** indicators are statistics that tell us where the business cycle has been recently, such as how much businesses spent on capital investments (equipment) and consumer credit levels.

- **Leading** indicators are statistics that show the direction in which the economy seems to be heading. Leading indicators of a recession might include falling stock prices, higher unemployment and lower housing starts. Leading indicators of a period of economic expansion might include a rising stock market, falling unemployment and more housing starts.

Some investors try to predict where the business cycle is heading and base their investing on timing the changes in the cycle. For example, during a growth phase in the economy, an investor might expect that the business cycle will reach a peak and then contract. Such a investor might stop buying stocks. In a recession, an investor might buy longer-term bonds to benefit from falling interest rates. Unfortunately, since we cannot accurately predict when the highs and the lows of the business cycle will occur, investors may move in and out of the market too early or too late.

Growth When business activity is expanding (sometimes also called the recovery phase since it often follows a recession and trough). Growth is measured by increased levels of production, employment and rising prices.

Peak When business activity is at its maximum level of production.

Recession When business activity is declining. This is a period of rising unemployment and declining production. If the decline in business activity is extreme, it may be referred to as a depression.

Trough When business activity is at its lowest level of production.

COMMON AND PREFERRED SHARES

There are two types of corporations that issue shares:

- Private corporations are companies whose stocks are not listed on any stock exchange or traded publicly. Often a private corporation is held by family shareholders or a small number of unrelated shareholders. There may have restrictions on who can own shares.
- Public corporations whose shares are listed on a public stock exchange or traded in over-the-counter markets.

Stocks in corporations come in two main categories, preferred shares and common shares:

- Preferred shares pay dividends at a fixed rate and their holders are legally entitled to receive their dividends before common shareholders (hence the term "preferred"), but they do not have the right to vote on issues related to running the company. Preferred share offerings of mature companies are often considered to be like a fixed-income investment because they have a guaranteed minimum dividend yield – rather than an equity investment. In the event the company goes bankrupt, preferred shareholders are paid before any common stock shareholders.
- Common shareholders are owners in the company. The shares they purchase represent not a loan, but an investment in the company's future that can be held as long as the company continues to offer them. The dividends received by common shareholders are based on a proportional share of after-tax profits of the corporation. Common shareholders are generally interested in the potential increased market value in the shares they hold. The dividends paid on common shares are not guaranteed and are usually lower than the dividend paid on preferred shares from the same company.

Preferred shares might have one or more of the following features. The features are designed to make the initial offering of the securities more attractive to prospective purchasers:

Convertible Includes the right to convert the preferred shares into common shares at a fixed price and time.

Callable Where the company can call in the shares. An investor should consider the date the shares can be called and the yield-to-call date to determine if the yield is competitive.

Retractable Redeemable by the shareholder at a fixed price and time. The shareholder can force the company to buy the shares back from the shareholder.

Floating rate preferred The stock dividend rate is linked to interest rates. If interest rates go up, the dividend payments go up. If interest rates go down, dividend payments go down.

Foreign-pay Canadian preferred shares issued in a foreign currency that pay dividends in that currency.

With a warrant Includes a right to purchase common stock using the warrant. Since the warrant can be detached from the stock and traded on its own, it is sometimes like receiving a bonus for purchasing the preferred share.

LARGE-CAP, MID-CAP AND SMALL-CAP

Stocks can also be classified by the market capitalization they have: the total market value of all the outstanding publicly traded shares they have issued. A company with 10 million outstanding shares with a current market value of $5 a share has a market capitalization of $50 million. While there is some overlap in the categories, the following definitions are generally followed:

- **Large-cap** companies generally have a market capitalization of over $1 billion. The stocks of large, established companies may have more price stability and be able to weather a downturn in the economy better than companies that are not as mature.

- **Mid-cap** companies have a market capitalization somewhere between a large- and a small-cap company.

- **Small-cap** companies are those valued between $25 million and up to $500 million, depending on the industry.

PENNY STOCKS

Penny stocks generally have a market price of under $1 a share. They often are associated with speculative companies still in the start-up phase. They are inherently risky, have a high failure rate and may have aggressive promotion.

However, no matter what the price of the stock or the age of a company, look carefully at the company to see if it stands up to your review of the

- business it is in. Is there the potential for a solid business or it is a stretch for anyone to see how this junior stock could ever strike it rich for its investors?
- promoters. Are they above board?

Occasionally a junior company turns out to be a leader in its industry and rewards its investors for the high risk they took.

If you don't want to follow closely those investments in your portfolio that have higher risk on a frequent basis, stay out of the riskier investments.

Some investors limit their investments to stocks that are household names. Historically, shares of brand-name companies, such as the major banks and utilities, have been favored.

STUDYING INDUSTRIES/SECTORS

Some people talk about the market as if it were one big market. What we really have is different markets in each country and then those markets are subdivided even further. In the United States, they have the NASDAQ to track indices for small companies, and the S&P 500, to name just two. In Canada, the Toronto Stock Exchange (TSE) tracks 14 sectors – each like its own market – and records the gains and losses for each industry subindex. These sectors include:

> Communications and media
> Conglomerates
> Consumer products
> Financial services
> Gold and precious metals
> Industrial products
> Merchandising
> Metals and minerals
> Oil and gas
> Paper and forest products
> Pipelines
> Real estate
> Transportation
> Utilities

Some weeks, all indices go up. In other weeks all go down, or some one way and the rest in the other direction. Some investors believe that changes in the resource sectors (gold, metals and oil and gas) foreshadow changes in other indices.

A portfolio that includes stocks from only one or two sectors is not well diversified.

Some investors select companies from sectors that they are particularly interested in or that seem to have good long-term growth potential. For example, an investor might be interested in the communications and high-tech sectors. If the investor picks a sector that is hot, he or she may earn higher than normal returns.

Stock markets have been described as **bulls** and **bears**.

 A bull market is one in which stock prices are generally rising and some investors underestimate the risks associated with investing.

 A bear market is one in which stock prices are generally falling. The generally accepted drop is 20 percent before a bear market is declared. The difference between a bear market and a "correction" is how severe it is and how long it lasts.

Some investors will head for the hills if they sense a bear coming.

RESEARCH, RESEARCH, RESEARCH

The major investment houses and mutual funds in Canada have research specialists assigned to various industries and companies. They study economic and corporate financial data, compare companies in similar industries and look for value that may not be reflected yet in the price of the stock. Or they seek out companies with strong earning potential that could outperform the market. Selecting stocks is their job and they use every resource available to help make educated decisions.

Even with all the research they have at their disposal, there is no guarantee brokers will always recommend companies with good fundamentals. Nor, in the case of mutual funds, will the managers always buy companies for their portfolios that make money. However, their research gives them a disciplined approach to selecting individual investments.

Sometimes an investor will stumble across a "rising star," a stock whose rise in price outperforms the market and attracts attention. Unfortunately, not all star stocks are supported by long-term company fundamentals. The Bre-X stock story of 1996–97 was an example of a rising star (for a time), where many investors made and lost much money.

In bull markets, it is sometimes said that all you have to do is buy some of the companies that are in the major stock indices and you have an instant, winning portfolio. But when we enter bear markets, picking the right stocks can give an investor better returns than the index (which might just mean you lose less than the index does).

Some investors choose to limit the stocks they buy and sell to the large blue chip companies, or companies that appear in the stock index. Certainly, this makes the universe of stocks from which to chose more manageable, but some investors select from these types of companies because they believe they are somehow safer. Remember, there is no such thing as a conservative stock – they go up and down in value. Even bank stocks and other stocks that have been described as investments for "widows and orphans" have been know to drop as much as 20 percent or more in a three-month period.

 If you are buying a house, the key to purchasing one that is most likely to maintain its price is "location, location, location." When investing, the mantra is "research, research, research."

There are those who believe investors who analyze companies and securities prices can earn higher returns. Market models often assume that there are a large number of rational investors who receive and react to the same information quickly. This is called the **efficient market theory**. However, nothing could be further from the truth. Some investors are paying attention to their portfolio on a daily (sometimes hourly) basis and others review their investments weekly or even monthly.

The starting point for analysis is to determine which stocks *not* to follow by eliminating those that perform below the average for their group or have obvious problems.

FUNDAMENTAL ANALYSIS

Fundamental analysis looks at the basics of both the business a company is in and its financial position. When looking at the business itself, the analyst considers the outlook for this type of business and the products it produces, how efficient the company is and its local and global competition.

Companies go through different stages in their development. When they are just starting out, the risk of failure is the highest, but so is the growth potential. In the growth phase a company may have rapid increases in corporate profits and sales. When the company is mature, it is expected to have more stable profits and sales. Eventually, some companies may decline and lose their market position.

When looking for good companies to invest in, you should look at the key financial information of a company:

- Are company revenue and sales increasing? Does it have new products coming to market? Is it expanding globally?
- Does the company have good cash flow to finance its operation and/or expansion? For example, if it doesn't have enough cash to service the interest payments on its debt, it could have a problem.
- What is the company's profitability? Is the company being operated efficiently?
- What is the company's profit margin? Is the company earning a reasonable return on equity (ROE) for a firm in its industry?
- What is the debt-to-equity ratio? Although the norm for this ratio varies from industry to industry, is there enough shareholder equity to balance against all debts, including bank debt and bond issues? A company with less debt tends to be higher quality than a firm in the same industry with higher debt.

- Is the company a leader in its industry?
- Does it have a focused business strategy? Or is the management trying to be all things to all investors?
- Does the company have good management? The key to running a profitable business is not just reflected in the financial numbers. The calibre of the company's management is an essential ingredient in the success of a business.

The question, of course, is how to access this information. Public companies are required to issue an annual report that can be obtained from their investor relations office. Awards are given each year for the best-looking annual report, but don't be swayed by the look of the report. The report will give you an overview of the mission and operations of the company, the financial and operational objectives for the coming years and some information about the industry the company operates in.

Studying a company's annual report and financial statements can provide investors with much information about the corporation. The financial statements include the balance sheet, statement of earnings, statement of retained earnings and statement of changes in financial position. They are also accompanied by a message from the chief executive officer or the president.

A balance sheet shows:

- the assets (what the company owns)
- the liabilities (what the company owes) and compares the current fiscal year-end with the previous fiscal year-end.

Simplified Balance Sheet for
Reading Unlimited Inc.

as of December 31 in 1000s of dollars

Assets

Current	Last Year-end	Previous Year-end
Cash	$ 6,128	$ —
Accounts receivable	6,117	4,199
Inventories	142,103	117,590
Prepaid expenses	3,087	2,536
Total current assets	157,435	124,325
Capital assets	56,710	36,504
Other	5,265	7,358
Total Assets	**$ 219,410**	**$ 168,187**

Liabilities and Shareholders' Equity

Current		
Bank indebtedness	$ —	$ 1,381
Accounts payable	95,461	72,895
Income taxes payable	1,430	3,265
Other	6,961	7,295
Total current liabilities	103,852	84,836
Long-term debt	11,125	31,208
Total Liabilities	**$ 114,977**	**$ 116,044**

Shareholders' Equity

Share capital	$ 98,800	$ 54,930
Retained earnings (deficit)	5,633	(2,787)
Total Shareholders' Equity	$ 104,433	$ 52,143
	$ 219,410	**$ 168,187**

One of the ratios you can calculate from the balance sheet is the working capital ratio or the current ratio, which will give you an idea of how much cash the company has to cover its short-term debt and obligations. The working capital ratio is:

$$\frac{\text{current assets}}{\text{current liabilities}}$$

From the above balance sheet, the working capital ratio for Reading Unlimited Inc. is $157,435/$103,852 = 1.52

One rule of thumb suggests that a company should have about two dollars of current assets, or cash, for each one dollar it owes.

Another useful ratio is the debt/equity ratio, which looks at the amount of debt a company owes in relation to the value of the shareholders' equity. The debt/equity ratio is:

$$\frac{\text{short- and long-term debt}}{\text{total shareholders' equity}}$$

From the above balance sheet, the debt/equity ratio is $114,977/$104,433, or slightly more than a one dollar of debt for every one dollar of shareholders' equity. Too much debt in relation to equity could indicate the company is on a shaky footing.

Of course, a look at the financial statements of a company goes beyond balance sheets. The investor must also look at the statement of earnings and the notes accompanying the financial statements.

To determine how much profit a company has made, the investor can look at the statement of earnings (sometimes called the profit and loss statement). The company's statement of earnings shows the income it generated and the expenses it paid out.

Statement of Earnings

for Reading Unlimited Inc.

as of December 31 in 1000s of dollars

Revenue	Current Year-end	Previous Year-end
Bookstores	$ 278,839	$ 308,062
Internet	177,772	81,704
	456,611	389,766
Cost of goods sold	423,707	364,252
	32,904	25,514
Amortization	13,907	10,613
Earnings before interest and taxes	18,997	14,901
Interest charges	2,627	4,751
Income taxes	7,950	5,080
Net earnings for the period	$ 8,420	$ 5,070
# of common shares outstanding	9,326	6,179
Basic earnings per share	$ .90	$ .82

Another key financial statement is the statement of retained earnings, which shows the portion of annual profit that was retained by the corporation (and not paid out as dividends).

Simplified Statement
of Retained Earnings

for Reading Unlimited Inc.

as of December 31 in 1000s of dollars

	Last Year-end	Previous Year-end
Deficit, beginning of period	$ (2,787)	$ (7,857)
Net earnings for the period	8,420	5,070
Retained earnings (deficit), end of period	$ 5,633	$ (2,787)

The statement of changes in financial position give you an inside look at the activities going on within the company and a look at how these compare with the previous year. This information can give you an idea of whether or not the firm is moving in the right direction with its cash and financing. From the statement on the next page, we can see that Reading Unlimited is improving its cash position and lowering its debt. This bodes well for future profits.

 Martin Pring says: "Fundamental analysis tells us how rational investors should behave, while technical analysis tells us how actual investors do behave."

Statement of Changes in Financial Position
for Reading Unlimited Inc.
as of December 31 in 1000s of dollars

	Last Year-end	Previous Year-end
Operating Activities		
Net earnings for period	$ 8,420	$ 5,070
Add (deduct) items not affecting cash		
Amortization	13,907	10,613
Deferred income taxes	2,109	3,107
Other		
	24,436	18,790
Net change in non-cash balances related to operations	(7,621)	(10,709)
Cash provided by operating activities	16,815	8,081
Cash used in investing activities	(32,176)	(14,493)
Cash from financing activities	22,870	25,408
Net increase in cash during period	7,509	18,996
Bank indebtedness, beginning of period	(1,381)	(20,377)
Cash (bank indebtedness), end of period	$ 6,128	$ (1,381)

In addition to the financial statements in the company's annual reports, many investors pay particular attention to the section of the annual report titled "notes to the financial statements." This section contains information that needs to be disclosed to the shareholders, but that cannot be reflected in the financial statements. The notes can indicate competitive strengths or weaknesses that will affect the financial strength and future earnings of the corporation.

When looking at the "notes to the financial statements," pay particular attention to changes in:

- accounting policies
- the nature of the business and/or operations as well as deferred liabilities, such as pension plan changes, any options senior officers or employees may have to acquire future shares, taxes and the nature of long-term debt

Analysts look at companies in the same industry to compare the relative strength of the different companies and the value of their stock. By looking at the financial data published in the corporate report, the investor and money manager can analyze the data and assess the operating costs of the business, its cash position, liabilities and profitability. This is called quantitative analysis. You can do the same thing by sending away for their annual reports and comparing companies within an industry. Traditionally, companies with good cash positions and low levels of debt are considered to have a stronger financial position than companies who do not, and can fare better than their competition if the economy faces a downturn or if interest rates rise.

TECHNICAL ANALYSIS

Investors use technical analysis to spot trends in the stock market based on price changes and trading volumes to help pinpoint when they should buy or sell a certain stock. These changes may or may not be based on the "fundamentals" (profits, etc.) of a company.

The major national newspapers provide weekly or monthly charts, but many investors crunch their own numbers by doing calculations on paper or using a computer and charting stock prices and trading volumes looking for investment trends and opportunities to make money. Many investors chart only companies they are interested in and have short-listed as ones they want to follow, not all the available investments. Technical analysis does not focus on changes in the business cycle or expected corporate earnings, but, of course, investors need to take these factors into consideration.

Investors might chart:

- closing prices from week to week, looking for trends that might indicate it is time to buy or sell.

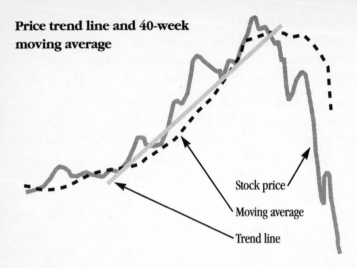

Price trend line and 40-week moving average

Stock price

Moving average

Trend line

To chart the price of a particular stock looking for a trend, the investor might graph the closing price for the stock from week to week and the **moving average** for that stock. A moving average is the average price of the stock over a period of time. The four-week moving average price of a stock would be calculated by adding up the closing price for the stock for the last four weeks and dividing by four.

The four-week moving average for the week ending July 28 would add the closing price for the weeks ending July 7, 14, 21 and 28 and divide the result by four. The four-week moving average for the week ending August 4 would be calculated by adding up the closing prices for the weeks ending July 14, 21, 28 and August 4 and dividing the result by four. Some analysts study prices over three months and longer, looking for a trend. This is what they study:

• **trading volumes** (the number of shares traded for a particular stock). Changes in trading volumes may affect the supply or the demand for shares of a particular company and a related change in the price of the stock. Rising volumes with a rising stock price may indicate an underlying demand for the stock, or perhaps a takeover attempt in the rumor mill. Falling volumes may indicate falling demand or a bear market around the corner.

Volume trend line and 40-week moving average

Moving average

Trend line

- **number of advances and declines**. You can look at the number of shares that increased in price and the number of shares that decreased in price and determine if there is trend developing. When there are more stocks trading with declining prices than trading with rising prices, it may be the forerunner of a bear market.

- **new highs and new lows**. A market is considered strong when the number of new highs is increasing and weak when the number of new lows is increasing.

- **changes in the TSE Index**. The TSE 300 Composite Index records changes in the stock prices of 300 key companies listed on the Toronto Stock Exchange. The companies and industries represent all major industry groups.

- **odd-lot transactions**. When the number of trades of odd-lot transactions is increasing, it is taken to mean that there are a number of small investors trading. Traditionally, smaller investors are thought to sell at the bottom of the market and buy at the top of the market, possibly indicating a current market trend is about to change direction.

- **changes in other indices** that report price trends within different sectors of the stock market. Price trends are reported in the industrial sector, gold sector, biotech or the financial sector, to name just a few.

 Investors often compare their individual performance with the appropriate index. Indices provide a benchmark rate of return, but they do not have to pay income tax, commissions or any expenses.

TSE 100 An index made up of 100 of Canada's largest companies.

EAFE Index An index of companies in Europe, Australia and the Far East.

MSCI World An index of the world equity markets, including the United States, maintained by Morgan Stanley Capital International.

S&P 500 An index of the 500 largest United States companies that represents all major industry sectors.

USE YOUR EYES

You don't have to be a Bay Street analyst to find a good company to buy. Sometimes, you just have to keep your eyes open. Someone bought the stock of a company because he was in the factory and noticed that every machine was working and the employees were complaining about the amount of overtime they were being asked to work. Sometimes, just paying attention to what is going on around you, then checking out the financial information of the company and the outlook for the industry it operates in helps you find a winning company.

BROKER RATINGS

Brokers base their stock selections on their own research and on their firm's research. For each stock on their list, the analysts at each firm have an opinion on whether that stock is a buy, hold or sell.

Stocks are classified as a *buy* when the analyst's research, be it fundamental, technical or a combination, indicates that the price of the stock will be heading upward. (Sometimes, a buy recommendation will be extended to share offerings that the firm is participating in.) If a broker recommends a stock as a buy, ask if his firm is underwriting a new issue for the company in question. If it is, be sure to step up the amount of due diligence you do before investing.

A stock is classified as a *hold* when the analyst may have previously recommended a stock as a buy, but no longer believes the outlook is promising. However, the analyst does not believe that it is necessary to sell the holdings at this time.

A stock classified as a *sell* may indicate that there has been some fundamental change in the outlook for the company and that shareholder value has fallen or is expected to drop.

It is sometimes more difficult for an investor to determine when to sell a stock than when to buy it. After all, if you decided it was a good investment, it may have to prove to you that it is a bad investment before you unload it – it's that emotional attachment that can lead to poor investment decisions. If you are tracking your investments as well as a few you would like to add to your portfolio you should be on the lookout for new investments that are likely to outperform one or two of your current holdings. Some people have a discipline that requires them to sell a stock position if it falls more than 10 percent below the price they paid for it, so they can cut their losses and move on.

You'll find that analysts at different firms may give the same stock different ratings. For example, in one week, some firms were listing stocks in the steel sector as a buy and others were listing the same stocks as a hold or a sell. Of course, you only get broker ratings from full-service brokerages or Internet services.

CHAPTER FOUR

Stock life cycle

INITIAL PUBLIC OFFERING

The first time a company issues shares to the public, it makes an initial public offering (IPO). The company is required, by securities law, to file a preliminary prospectus that discusses the company and the reasons it is raising money. Investors read the information regarding the company and its offering – and the fine print – found in the prospectus. Sometimes this will be a good opportunity for you, sometimes not.

The **prospectus** is a document required by securities law that describes the securities being offered for sale for the first time. The prospectus discloses the facts that are considered material for the investor to make an informed decision:

- the details of the stock offering – including the price and the details of the type of security offered
- information on the business – including the company name, its operations, the names of the company's directors and officers
- details of the promoters of the initial offering
- financial information on the company – including financial statements, balance sheet and history of dividend payments
- any risks related to the investment

This document should provide you with all the facts of the company before you choose to invest your money. A **preliminary prospectus** is sometimes issued in advance of the final prospectus, but no sales can be made based on this document because it does not contain all the material facts.

If you are considering investing in a new company or new stock issue, be sure to request and read the prospectus and understand the potential risks and outlook for the company before investing. The issuance of a prospectus does *not* imply the securities commission has an opinion on the quality of the security itself.

An investor purchasing a new stock issue has two legal rights defined in the prospectus:

- the right of rescission, or cancelling of the purchase, if the prospectus contains an untrue or misleading statement
- the right to withdraw from a purchase agreement within two business days after receiving the final prospectus

The prospectus is designed to provide you with the information you need to make an informed decision regarding a new share offering by providing "true, plain and full" disclosure regarding the company and the details of the offering. After the initial offering, the stocks will trade in the public market, either on a listed stock exchange or in the over-the-counter market, and the financial information of the company will be published in the annual report and any pertinent information will be disclosed in a timely manner to all investors and to the general public, often through press releases.

The brokerage house introducing a new issue may be acting as an agent for the company raising money through the stock issue, or it may have a **bought deal**, where the brokerage firm buys the stocks and turns around to resell them to the public. If the dealer buys the new issue in a falling market, the firm will lose money on the deal. In a rising market, the firm stands to profit.

STOCK TRANSACTIONS

Once a stock is issued, there are a number of transactions that could affect all current shareholders:

Stock split When the price of a stock goes up, it might get into the range where new investors feel it is too expensive. Suppose a stock increases in value to $75 and a five-for-one split is approved. Each holder of one share at $75 would receive five shares valued initially at $15.

Stock consolidation This is the opposite of a stock split. Suppose the price of a stock has fallen and the shareholders approve a consolidation of one new share for five old shares. If each old share was worth one dollar, each new share would be valued initially at five dollars.

Dividend declared This is done by the directors of the corporation and is paid to all the registered shareholders.

Share exchange or stock swap Sometimes the shares are exchanged for the shares of another class or other company. This could be the result of a name change or the merger of two companies.

Trading halt This is ordered by the stock exchange to allow time for a news flash to be distributed, such as a management announcement.

Delisted This happens when the company is removed from the trading list or the stock exchange for not meeting certain requirements or if the company goes bankrupt.

Corporate buy backs When the company uses some of its cash to purchase its own shares back from individual investors, usually without commission being charged. The company may consider that the stock is undervalued. When the number of outstanding shares decreases, the price of the remaining shares sometimes goes up in value and the future dividend obligations decrease.

MERGERS, ACQUISITIONS, TAKEOVERS, BUYOUTS

Companies occasionally merge with one another. For example, in 1998, two of the major banks in Canada proposed merging into one bank to be more competitive in the global marketplace and, of course, lower the fees they charge their customers. Initially, this pushed up the price of their shares.

Sometimes, the company in which you own shares may become the target of a **takeover bid**, where the owners of one company try to obtain controlling ownership in another. As the shareholder, you would receive information regarding the details of the takeover and a comment from current management regarding their response to the offer. You may be asked to respond to the offer within a certain number of days. In late 1998, Torstar offered to take over SunMedia, but it was described as a hostile takeover bid because SunMedia wanted no part of it.

If the takeover is successful, then your shares may automatically be redeemed for cash or some shares of the new company.

A company may want to buy the shares of another company, but may lack the capital to do so. Occasionally they may borrow money to buy the shares of the target company in what is called a **leveraged buyout**. The takeover company must ensure they can afford to carry the cost of the loan.

AT THE END OF THE DAY

What every investor wants to avoid is owning worthless stock. Companies are not always well managed. Companies, like individuals, occasionally get in over their heads and are unable to pay their bills. When a company goes bankrupt, you could end up with shares that are worthless (except maybe as wallpaper).

By doing research and keeping an eye on what the companies you own are up to, you can help ensure that they continue to be viable business operations, and not a capital loss for you to claim on your tax return.

CHAPTER FIVE

Opening an account

To place an order to buy a stock, you have to open an account with a brokerage, a firm that deals in securities. The investment industry is highly regulated and each firm has to be registered with a securities exchange; each sales representative also has to be registered with the securities exchange. The person you deal with may be called a stockbroker, account executive, financial consultant, financial advisor or registered representative.

Your first decision will be to determine if you need the services of a full-service broker or a discount broker.

DISCOUNT VERSUS FULL-SERVICE BROKER

Canadians can choose between the services of a full-service broker and a discount broker. Some investors prefer to have a broker who can provide them with investment advice and the full range of investments available, including stocks, bonds and mutual funds. If this is you, you will need to work with someone from a full-service firm registered to sell securities. They may also provide you with a financial planning framework to help you set and achieve your financial goals.

Other people are experienced investors and have the time to do the research required. If this is you, you may prefer to use the limited services provided by a discount broker and do your trading more cheaply than you could with a full-service broker. A discount broker is there primarily to take your order.

The Internet has been a boon to the do-it-yourself investor, providing access to online research and low-cost trading. Of course, you need to be sure that the site you deal with provides bona fide research and has adequate security to protect both your money and your privacy. It is difficult for the securities regulators to monitor the investment information posted online and more than one investor has been the victim of a "cyber-scam." You should consider the source of any information you receive over the Internet and you may want to focus on Internet sites provided by sources you can identify. Each major bank and trust company has an Internet research and/or trading facility. Other Internet sites with solid reputations are:

> www.canada.etrade.com
> www.prioritybrokerage.com

Both discount brokers and full-service brokers qualify for coverage with the Canadian Investor Protection Fund.

The services provided by discount brokerage online continue to grow and may include:

* reviewing historical performance charts
* tracking your portfolio performance
* entering your buy and sell orders electronically
* up-to-the-minute stock quotes
* receiving messages when your stocks reach target prices for buying or selling
* online research

Regardless of where you place your trades, research – and a bit of luck – is key to picking good companies. If you need some assistance and guidance, some discount brokerages have advisory services there to help you.

While there are few guarantees that protect you from losing money in the financial markets, there are two types of protection for investors:

- Canada Deposit Insurance Corporation (**CDIC**) protects the **cash** deposits of an investor up to $60,000. For example, if you had cash and certificates of deposit with Confederation Life Insurance Company when it went under in the early '90s, the Canada Deposit Insurance fund would have paid up to $60,000.
- The Canadian Investor Protector Fund (**CIPF**) was set up to protect investors if their brokerage went under. The CIPF protects investors for up to $500,000 for **securities** held in an account with a firm registered with one of the major exchanges or the Investment Dealers Association (IDA), but does not cover losses resulting from changes in the market value of investments. Each brokerage pays a premium each year into the fund.

Some firms have insurance coverage above the CIPF limits.

THE CLIENT APPLICATION

To open an investment account, you will be required to provide some personal information, including your income, net worth, family situation, where you work and so on. This is part of the "know your client" rules the financial industry follows.

The client application will also describe the amount of risk you are willing to assume. The form may describe the risk level as income, growth or aggressive growth, or it may indicate the percentage of your portfolio that you are prepared to hold in income investments, growth investments or in investments aimed at aggressive growth.

You will probably want to make your own decisions regarding your account. This means the broker needs to contact you and obtain your approval before a transaction is made. If you give discretionary authority to the broker, he or she can make investment decisions for your account without consulting you prior to a transaction. If you set up a discretionary account, there should be clear, written guidelines as to the type of trading activity that is appropriate for the account.

TYPES OF INVESTMENT ACCOUNTS

There are three types of investment accounts you can hold:

- **Cash account** or a non-registered account. In a cash account, investors pay for their stock investments in full on the settlement date, which is normally three days for stocks and bonds, one day for money market investments. For mutual fund investments, most companies require that they have your cheque in hand, or cash, before they will place an order.

- **Margin account**, where the brokerage firm is willing to extend credit to the investor to buy the investments – with some money down. You are actually borrowing money from the brokerage firm and have to pay interest. The firm uses the stocks or other investments as collateral for the loan. For example, if the share price of a stock is over five dollars, the brokerage firm may extend margin credit of up to 70 percent of the market value of the investment. If the value of the security goes up, the brokerage firm may be willing to extend you more credit. If the value of the security goes down, the firm may make a margin "call" and require you to add more cash to your account. If you don't, they will sell some investments in the account to cover the margin call, possibly at a loss to you.

- **Registered RRSP** and **RRIF** accounts, which work much like a cash account except that the trustee has to follow the rules for registered plans and report contributions, withdrawals and foreign content to Revenue Canada. The RRSP could be your own, a spousal account or a locked-in RRSP account. RRSP and RRIF accounts that hold individual stocks are normally self-directed.

A full-service broker may charge a trustee fee of up to $125 per year for a self-directed RRSP or RRIF. A discount broker may waive the trustee fee or discount it sharply.

ACCOUNT STATEMENTS

If your account is with a full-service dealer or discount broker, you will receive account statements at least every quarter, and each month when there are transactions in the account.

Every investment company produces its own statement, in its own format. The statement will include:

- general information identifying the account number, account type and your name
- a summary of the holdings in your portfolio as of the date the statement is prepared
- a listing of all of the transactions in your account since the last statement date

Always review your account statements and match them with the confirmations you receive during the statement period for account activities. If there is any transaction on your statement that you did not authorize, be sure to investigate it.

COMMISSIONS CHARGED

The commission charged for a trade will depend on the service the brokerage house provides and their commission schedule. A full-service broker may have a minimum commission of $75 and up, depending on the number of shares traded and the total value of the trade. A discount broker my charge a flat fee for trades done through the Internet, as little as $20 or less, or a fee based on the value of the trade.

DO YOU NEED A FULL-SERVICE BROKER?

More than one person has decided that they can renovate their house without professional advice to save some money, only to end up paying more because they learned through trial and error. Similarly, when investing, you need to research your investments, and make sure that you are incorporating tax planning so you keep as much of your profits as possible.

Studies have shown that small investors tend to buy stocks that follow the overall trend of the market, wait for a stock to show an upward direction before buying and often trade too much. The transaction costs reduce their profits.

CHANGING BROKERS

It is relatively easy to move your account from one financial institution to another once you have selected the firm and the broker you want to work with.

You can move your account in cash or "in kind," which means all the investments you currently hold in your account are transferred from one financial institution to another. But beware. Your account will be in limbo for a brief period of time while the shares are being reregistered.

 If you are transferring an RRSP or RRIF from one broker to another, there may be a transfer fee of up to $125 plus GST. If you are transferring an open or margin account, there may be a transfer fee of up to $100 plus GST. The discount broker receiving your account may be willing to rebate your transfer fee or to cover the first year's trustee fee once the account is in their care.

COMPLAINTS

If you believe your broker has treated you unfairly or dishonestly, you should bring your concerns to your broker's attention. If you do not receive a satisfactory response, then report the situation to the branch manager or to the firm's compliance officer in writing. If the complaint is serious, you may also want to lodge a written complaint with the Investment Dealers Association and/or the provincial stock exchange. Your letter should include:

- the name of the brokerage firm
- the name of the broker you dealt with
- the details of the problem, including the date of the transaction and the security traded
- your name, address and phone number

These are typical complaints made by investors about their brokers:

- recommendation of an investment that is not suitable for their situation and objectives
- trades made for their account without authorization
- misleading information regarding the investment
- loans they made to their broker
- excess trading in their account
- excessively high commissions charged
- guarantees that cannot be met, such as "you'll double your money in four months"
- high-pressure sales practices

CHOOSING THE RIGHT BROKER FOR YOU

Brokers will help you select the stocks for your portfolio. But they may not be able to do better than you could do on your own. Some brokers specialize in value companies, others in growth companies and others in speciality sectors such as telecommunications and resources. Some brokers can also offer financial planning services to help you minimize your tax bill and meet your investment objectives.

There are a number of designations that a broker can earn, including CIM, Canadian Investment Manager, and FCSI, Fellow of the Canadian Securities Institute. The FCSI designation requires a minimum of five years of experience as well as industry-specific examinations.

When selecting a broker, you should take the time to interview to determine if the broker is willing to listen to what you need and whether or not you feel comfortable dealing with the individual and the firm he or she is associated with. You should also find out how much experience the broker has, including experience in navigating through difficult financial markets.

CHAPTER SIX

Buying stocks

Once you have researched which stocks you are interested in and have opened an account with a broker, you are ready to place your order to buy the shares of a particular company.

You could build a portfolio with a dozen stocks or 100 stocks. But once you own them, you have to be prepared to continue to research them to determine if you should keep holding them, or if you would be better to sell them and replace them with companies that have better prospects.

Stocks in Canada can be listed on one of the public stock exchanges or traded in the over-the-counter market. Canada has six stock exchanges: Montreal (ME), Alberta (ASE), Vancouver (VSE), Toronto (TSE), Calgary, and Winnipeg. Some stocks are listed on only one exchange, some are listed on more than one in Canada and the United States. Transactions in the **over-the-counter** (OTC) market are primarily handled over the phone, rather than through electronic trading, where the dealer matches the buyer and the seller. On the major stock exchanges, the transactions are entered electronically and all interested buyers or sellers are informed at the same time.

READING THE STOCK TABLES

The major national newspapers offer daily stock tables (published Tuesday to Saturday) for stocks listed on the different stock exchanges. There is a different listing for each exchange. Your paper may print a stock table for each exchange across the country or the stock tables for selected exchanges only.

Only stocks traded on public exchanges are listed, and usually only those stocks most actively traded. Since the price of a stock can change many times during a day, these tables provide data that can indicate what has happened. The data in the quotation tables can also help you determine current prices and some relative statistics, such as price-to-earnings ratios and dividend yields, of various companies. But before buying or selling a particular security, be sure to get an up-to-date quote.

The stock tables in the financial pages appear in varying formats, but you may have to get out your magnifying glasses to be able to read them! In your newspaper, there should be a key called "How to read the stock tables" that you can refer to. Here's a sampling of the information that could be listed in your paper and how to read it.

Stock Quote Table ① ② ③ ④ ⑤ ⑥ ⑦ ⑧ ⑨

| 52-week | | | | | | | | 000s | % | P/E |
high	low	Stock	Symbol	Div	Bid	Ask	Close	Chg	Vol.	Yield	Ratio
44.25	26.88	BCE Inc.	BCE	1.36	40.15	39.65	39.5	-0.30	100	3.43	23.2
24.45	12.05	CanWest	CGS.A	.25	23.35	23.00	23.1	-0.25	300	1.07	24.8
41.75	22.53	CIBC	CM	1.00	38.25	37.30	37.7	-0.70	200	2.67	11.7
25.10	24.00	CIBC	CM.PR.E	0.82	24.7	24.7	24.7	0.0	100	3.32	

(The companies in this table were selected at random.)

Each stock is listed in alphabetical order by stock name (2) and its stock code for trading purposes.

In the **dividend** column (3), any dividends declared in the 12 months are reported. From the above table, you can see that BCE Inc. paid a dividend of $1.36 for an effective yield of 3.43 percent.

Shareholders on record as of the date the dividend is declared are entitled to receive the dividend payment. The stock price quote may be **ex dividend** or **cum dividend**. If the stock price is shown as ex dividend, the new purchaser will *not* receive a dividend that has been declared – the seller is entitled to receive that dividend. Otherwise, the new purchaser will receive a dividend that has been declared but not yet paid.

The bid and ask columns (4) show the prices at which investors are willing to buy and sell the security. The **bid** reports the highest amount anyone was willing to pay for the shares. The **ask** amount is the lowest anyone was willing to sell shares at. In Canada, prices are quoted to the nearest five cents. Many international stock markets have also converted to a decimal system.

The **closing** column (5) shows the stock price at the close of trading. The **change** column (6) indicates in change in the price from the close of trading on the previous day. The volume column (7) shows the number of shares bought and sold the previous day. The dividend **yield** (8) on the stock is based on the price of the stock and is calculated as:

$$\frac{\text{annual dividend per share}}{\text{current market price per share}} \times 100$$

The high and low (1) columns report the trading range for the stock over the previous 52 weeks.

From the previous table, as of the close of business the day before the table was prepared, CanWest was trading in the range of $23.00 to $23.35 per share; 300,000 shares were traded and at the close of business, the shares were trading around $23.10, down 25 cents from the price the previous day. The dividend yield for CanWest was 1.08 percent 0.25 divided by 23.00) And over the last 52 weeks, CanWest has traded as high as $24.45 and as low as $12.05 per share.

The P/E ratio or P/E multiple (9) can be useful for comparing one company with other companies in the same industry. Comparing P/E ratios for companies in completely different industries has limited value, if any. Some growth stocks have little or no earning expectations in the short term. The P/E ratio is calculated as:

$$\frac{\text{current market price per share}}{\text{company's earnings per share}}$$

From the previous table the P/E ratio for Canwest was 24.8 percent which was calculated using the current market price per share of $23.10 and the company's earnings per share taken from the company's financial statements as disclosed in the annual report.

A low P/E ratio may represent a value stock. A higher P/E ratio may represent a growth stock, or just a stock that is overpriced. Some of the technology stocks have had their prices increase in value, at the same time as when little or no revenues are expected.

PLACING YOUR ORDER

For every stock that is sold by a determined seller, there is a patient buyer on the other side of the transaction who is willing to buy that stock. These two people may have entirely different opinions on the outlook for the stock, but they can't both be right.

Stocks are bought and sold in the financial markets through a stock exchange or in over-the-counter markets. A stock exchange is a formalized financial market with rules all participants must follow. It is operated by a group of investment dealers, who create the environment where stocks can be traded. Securities used to be bought and sold on behalf of investors by traders who would stand in a "pit" and make the deals. Over the years, open pit trading has been replaced by electronic trading in most markets.

The seller's order to sell a security is matched to a buyer's order to purchase a particular security. If there are no offers to buy the security at the price it is offered, the seller may need to lower the price to attract a buyer.

If you decide you want to buy or sell shares of a particular company, you need to place an order through a broker or discount broker represented on the stock exchange. The broker will charge a commission. Commissions are a percentage of the order, or are based on the number of shares traded and the trade price.

There is normally a minimum commission charged. If the order is relatively small, the commission may be relatively high. Since commissions are charged when shares are purchased and again when shares are sold, investors should consider how much the stock has to go up in value just to cover the commission costs. Suppose you are considering 100 shares priced at $10 per share with a minimum commission cost of $75. The commission charged to buy the stock (and again to sell the stock) would be:

$$\frac{\$75}{\$1,000} \ \text{x} \ 100 = 7.5\%$$

Your stock would have to go up in value by 15 percent just to cover the commission costs of buying and selling the stock, before you can even start to take any profits. If you purchase the stock for a selling commission of $25, the stock would only have to increase by 5 percent before you would start to take any profits.

To buy or sell a stock, your broker will ask for these five items:

- the name of the stock
- the number of shares you want to buy or sell
- if you're willing to buy or sell a partial number of shares or if you must deal with all the shares at once
- the price at which you're willing to buy or sell (or simply "best market price")
- how long your order is to stay in effect

The name of the stock Some companies have many classes of preferred and common stock, each with a slightly different trading code.

The number of shares you want to buy or sell A board lot is a standard trading unit for shares. The number of shares in a board lot depends on the trading price of the share and the exchange it is listed on. For example, on the Toronto Stock Exchange, the number of shares in a board lot for securities trading for more than 10 cents a share:

Share price	*Number of shares in a board lot*
less than $1	500 shares
$1 and over	100 shares

A trading order that is not equal to a board lot is called an odd lot and the commission charged may be higher for an odd lot than for a board lot, unless the commission is a flat fee.

What to do if the broker cannot fill all your order You may specific your order as "all or none" if you want your order to filled entirely, or not at all. Sometimes you may be able to buy part of your order even if you cannot get all the shares you want. You might want to state that if someone is willing to sell you part of the shares you are looking for, then you want the order to be filled. If you want the order to be cancelled as soon as any part of it has been filled, this is called a *fill and kill order*.

The price Your broker will want to know if you want to sell or buy the shares at a **specific price** or if you want the **best market price** available when the order is placed. You can also put in a stop-loss order on a particular stock if you want the stock to be sold if the market price falls below a certain price.

You can specify the maximum price you are willing to pay (or the price to sell) a stock, which is called the *limit price*. Your order will only be executed if the securities can be traded at that price or at a better price. If you do not specify the amount you are willing to pay for your stock, it will be filled at the best *market price* at the time the order is placed by your broker. When market is very active or volatile, some brokers recommend that you place your order with a limit price, to avoid selling at too low a price, or buying at too high a price. Some days, the TSE 300 can swing 300 points or more in one direction or the other.

It is always a good idea to get the current trading price for the stock minutes prior to placing the order.

How long your order is to stay in effect When you place your order, you can specify how long you want the purchase order to be open or pending. If nothing is specified, the purchase order automatically expires at the end of the day. Orders might not be filled if no one is willing to sell you the shares you were interested in. You may want to place an order that will last longer than a day, while you are waiting for someone who is willing to sell you their stock at a price you are willing to pay. This is called an *open order* or a *good until cancelled order*.

People who own stocks used to receive a stock certificate. Today, most people own stocks without ever receiving one. Instead, they own the stock in street name, which facilitates the clearance and settlement of transactions. A stock registered in street name is registered on your behalf through your brokerage and appears on your statement that the brokerage produces. If the stock splits or the company is taken over, the broker does all the paperwork. And you don't have to worry about physically delivering the share certificates to your broker when you want to sell because they are already in your account. If you receive a stock certificate, you are responsible for keeping it safe, responding to investor notices and delivering the certificate to your broker when you want to sell.

Suppose, for instance, you want to buy the stock of a Canadian bank. You have to place the order by phone or using the Internet. To place an order, you have to specify:

- how many shares of the stock you want to buy
- the price you are willing to pay for them
- how long you want to wait until the order is filled

You will receive a written confirmation from the order desk of the brokerage through which you placed the order to buy or sell stock. The confirmation will state:

- the date the order was filled
- the security traded
- the transaction price and the number of shares bought or sold
- the amount of commission charged for the trade
- the amount required to settle the trade

When settlement dates were five days, brokerage firms were willing to execute a trade and have you deliver the cash (for a purchase order) or the securities (for a sale) within the settlement period. Now that settlement dates are three days, some brokerage firms require you to have the cash in your account (or a margin account) before making a purchase, or that you deliver the securities before they will execute a sale order on your behalf.

SELLING A STOCK

Some investors find it easier to select a new stock for their portfolio than to determine when they should sell a stock they already have in their portfolio. If your analysis still tells you that the stock is of good quality and you don't need the money, maybe you don't need to sell it. But if your analysis suggests that you would be better off selling this stock and replacing it with another, determine the taxes that would be due from a sale before proceeding.

Where there are few investors who are willing to buy or sell the stock of a single company, the market for that stock is described as being **thinly traded**. The price from one transaction to the next may have larger swings in prices than a stock that has more investor interest.

SHORT SELLING

When investors buy a stock, they generally are hoping that the stock will go up on value. Shorting a stock, or short selling, is hoping that a stock will go down in value. It works this way: you sell the stock before you buy it and cover the short position by buying back the shares when the price falls.

To make short selling work, an investor looks for companies with inflated stock prices, or major problems in their management or operations. When you find one you like, you place a "short sell."

BORROWING TO INVEST: LEVERAGE AND MARGIN ACCOUNTS

Borrowing to invest, using other people's money, can enhance an investor's returns, but it also **magnifies** the amount that can be lost in a down market. For example, if you can borrow money at 5 percent and make 15 percent in the stock market, you can invest more and possibly make more than you could on your own. However, if you borrow to invest and the stock market falls by 15 percent and you also have to repay the interest on the loan, your personal loss will be greater than 15 percent.

At one time, investors who used borrowed money to invest mainly did it through margin accounts at the brokerage house. Credit could be extended to investors as long as there were sufficient assets in the account to cover the loan, otherwise their broker would "call" the loan. Now, Canadians can borrow money conveniently through lines of credit and personal loans to invest without using the investments as collateral. And in the right circumstances, you can deduct the interest paid.

IS BORROWING TO INVEST A GOOD IDEA?

Most Canadians would not own their own home if they had not been able to borrow money (in the form of a mortgage) to help finance the purchase. So borrowing has its merits. When market are going up, borrowing money to invest can increase your profits. However, when markets are going down, borrowing money magnifies your loss. Even if your investment loan is not tied to the value of your investments, ensure that you can afford the loan payments even if the value of your investments goes down. The key to using borrowed money for any purpose is to use it wisely.

OPTIONS

Options might best be left for experienced investors, but let's take a look at them so you can understand what they are and how they might be used for investing.

When you buy a stock, you physically purchase it. Money is exchanged for the full value of the stock and you are said to have a *long* position. An option is a contract that gives you the right to buy or sell securities in the future, at a price you negotiate when you buy the option contract. When you buy a *call contract*, you pay for the option contract, which gives you the right to buy the stock at a pre-agreed price. Buyers of call options believe the price of the stock will rise.

When you buy a *put contract*, you pay for an option contract, which gives you the right to sell stock at a pre-agreed price. Buyers of put options believe the price of the stock will fall and must be prepared to actually sell the stock, if the option is exercised.

MEASURING PORTFOLIO PERFORMANCE

Tracking the performance of your portfolio and of your individual investments will help you determine if your returns are sufficient to help you achieve your investment objectives, such as retiring at a certain age, or having enough money to put your children through school. If you have done a retirement independence calculation to estimate how much you need to earn (or how much you have to save each year to have the retirement income you want when you want it), you know you have to make some assumptions as to the rate of return your investments will earn.

When you are tracking your performance, be sure to include the change in the price of your securities, the capital growth, as well as any dividend income that was paid.

 Do not include any additional savings you added to your account in your performance figures.

You may want to track the performance of your portfolio annually, monthly, weekly or more often. Investors often use benchmark returns to measure how they are doing. Canadian stock investors might compare their annual returns with the TSE 300; international investments to the Morgan Stanley Capital International Index, the MSCI World Index. The higher the risk in your investments, the higher the long-term returns you should expect to receive. But remember, a portfolio with higher risk could have higher losses than a more conservative portfolio in any short-term period. You can't hope to win big unless you are also prepared to lose big.

OTHER WAYS TO BUY STOCKS

In addition to buying individual stocks through a stock broker, investors can participate in the stock market in other ways.

Dividend reinvestment programs (DRIP) Offered by a limited number of major Canadian corporations. When dividends are declared, they are normally paid out as a cash payment to the investor. Some companies, however, give their shareholders the option of using the cash from the dividend payment to purchase additional shares, with no commission charged to the shareholder. Some companies also allow shareholders who are participating in the dividend reinvestment plan to purchase additional shares using other cash, up to certain limits.

By buying additional shares on a regular basis through a dividend reinvestment program, investors can increase their holdings in a company they have already selected based on its role in their portfolio and financial outlook.

Holders of rights and warrants also participate in the stock market. Rights may be offered when a stock is initially offered to the public to increase the sales of the stock with a lower price. Holders of rights are entitled to buy more shares at a fixed price with no commission prior to their expiry date and may want to exercise their right when the fixed price is lower than the current market price.

Holders of warrants have benefits similar to holders of rights. However, some warrants give the holder the option to buy other financial instruments, such as a future bond issue, something other than shares in the corporation.

Rights and warrants listed on the stock exchange can be traded.

Buying stocks through employment If you work for a company that has stocks listed on a public stock exchange, one of your employee benefits may be a share purchase plan. These employee plans work in a number of different ways, but essentially they allow employees to acquire stock in the company through payroll deduction on a no-commission basis. Sometimes the company will match up to 100 percent of the employee's savings rate. Periodically, the shares will be deposited to the employee's account or share certificates issued.

Buying TIPS or other indices that trade like stocks Investors who do not want to make individual investments on the Toronto Stock Exchange, but who want to participate in the changes in the stock market, could buy units in TIPS. Ideally for passive investors, TIPS 35 invests in a basket of 35 of the largest companies on the Toronto Stock Exchange and its performance is expected to follow the direction of the TSE. Active investors usually want to try to outperform the index.

When the stock market is booming, the index might outperform most mutual funds, since it has no trading costs and minimal expenses. But when the stock market is falling, the index will also fall and may underperform other investment opportunities.

The value of a TIPS unit is based on the value of the stocks of the 35 companies that make up the index. If the market goes up, then the value of a TIPS unit should increase. If the market goes down, the value of a TIPS unit will fall. TIPS units are listed in the financial pages in Toronto stock tables.

Mutual funds or segregated funds Mutual funds are a way of packaging individual securities for investors and are managed by professional money managers. If you purchase a mutual fund, your money is pooled with other investors' money and you are effectively hiring the services of a professional money manager. If you invest in a Canadian equity mutual fund, the money manager is selecting Canadian companies on your behalf. (Segregated funds are also a form of professionally managed funds that are sold or packaged by Canadian life insurance companies.)

There are Canadian equity funds that focus on:

- companies that pay dividends
- stock selection on a value basis
- stock selection on a growth basis
- sector rotation
- specific industries, such as financial or resources
- and more

Management fees are charged for researching, selecting the investments to buy and determining when to select certain invest ments in the portfolio – for the professional money management. When the fund is making money, management fees and the expenses of the fund are charged against the returns the fund makes. Even when the fund is not making money for the investor, the money managers and the expenses still get paid, effectively out of the assets of the fund. The management expense ratio varies from 0.75 percent to over 3.5 percent.

Some investors buy and sell shares of closed-end mutual funds listed on a stock exchange at a discount or a premium to the value of the assets in the fund. A closed-end fund trades in a manner similar to the way the shares of a corporation would be traded.

When an investor holding shares wishes to buy units, he or she must find an investor who is willing to sell his or her units. When an investor wishes to sell his or her units, a buyer must be found through the stock market.

Wrap accounts In addition to the professional money management offered by mutual funds, professional money management is also available through wrap accounts. The minimum investment required for wrap accounts is normally $100,000, and the annual fees are based on a percentage of the assets under management.

Index-linked GICs Index-linked, or equity-linked, GICs give savers (or those who are afraid to risk their capital) the chance to share in the growth of a stock market. The rate of return depends on the stock markets the GIC is linked to. Some are linked to one of the Canadian indices; some are linked to one or more international indices.

These GICs guarantee to return no less than your original capital, but they cannot be redeemed before their maturity date.

Investment counselling Investment counselling services are available to clients with larger portfolios. Annual fees of 1 percent or more are charged for the on-going investment management.

CHAPTER SEVEN

International investing

Canada has less than 3 percent of the world's financial markets, and some of the world largest companies are not listed on the Canadian stock exchanges. Investors often look beyond Canadian borders for investment opportunities and hope to find companies in foreign countries with greater growth potential than those at home.

Historically, global investments have tended to move in different cycles than the Canadian market. As an example, Japan has often been up in value when Canada was down in value. But recent market corrections have reminded us how closely connected activities on one side of the world are to those on the other side and the impact falling markets in Asia can have on stock markets in North America.

Nonetheless, international investing has its appeal for potentially higher returns. But while international investing as part of a broadly diversified portfolio is believed to reduce the overall risk of the total portfolio, the international investor should have an above-average tolerance for risk, because there are added currency fluctuations, political uncertainty and economic risk. If you are purchasing stocks on foreign exchanges, you also have to deal with potential language barriers and the tax laws of another country. It may be more difficult to get the information you require to make an informed investment decision, but there are a growing number of sites on the Internet providing quality information.

As an international investor, you may want to:

- have a well-diversified portfolio of stocks around the world
- focus on a particular country or region of the world that is either well established or is an emerging region

International investments can be made in individual investments, using indices, or international mutual funds. Just like someone investing in Canada can choose between blue chip stocks and small growing companies, the Canadian investor abroad can also choose. But you can further choose between well-established economies of the world and those of emerging regions. Of course, the emerging regions have more risk than the well-established economies, but like emerging companies, may also have greater reward.

Country-specific mutual funds

There are a number of mutual funds, open and closed-end funds, that focus on the companies in a specific country. If you like the prospects for Germany, you would focus on a German fund. If you like Japan, you would focus on a Japanese fund.

Just as with any mutual fund, there are management fees and the quality of the manager is important. Some managers "manage" from their own country, with barely a trip to the country in which they are investing. Other managers take regular trips (and not just for their vacations) to research and take on-site tours of the companies currently in their portfolio, or that they are considering added to their portfolio.

Each industrialized country of the world has its own economy and stock market. For example, the outlook for the United States economy and the direction of the U.S. dollar sets the stage for investment in American business. The outlook for the European economy will set the stage for investment in that region of the world.

71

When you invest in companies outside Canada, you are buying stocks listed on the stock markets of foreign countries. Other countries may report their financial data differently or use standards that are different from those used in Canada, so you may not be able to directly compare the financial results of a company in Europe with a company in a similar business in Canada.

LISTINGS ON MULTIPLE EXCHANGES

Some stocks are listed on more than one exchange. For example, some Canadian companies are listed on both the Toronto Stock Exchange (TSE) and in New York. If you are interested in buying a company listed on both exchanges, you will have to decide where to buy it. Canadian investors who select a company but also want to increase their U.S. currency holdings might buy it out of New York in U.S. dollars. Someone who is more concerned with the tax treatment of the dividends they receive might prefer to buy the company on the Toronto Stock Exchange. Or if they are buying it for their RRSP, they might buy it on the TSE and use their foreign content for investments that they could not buy any other way.

In Canada, you can place an order to buy a stock listed on a U.S. stock exchange as easily as you can for a stock listed on a Canadian stock exchange.

ADRs (American depositary receipts) are shares of non-U.S. companies that are issued by U.S. banks and trade like other stocks. Some of the most well-known international companies trade as ADRs in the U.S. The stocks of these companies may not be registered with the securities commission in the United States. ADRs allow you to purchase the shares of foreign companies on the U.S. exchanges, which is simpler than buying the shares of a company on an international exchange because you don't have to worry about currency conversions (except to U.S. dollars) and issues of international tax.

U.S. AND INTERNATIONAL STOCK INDICES

Canadian investors who want to investing in U.S. indices in U.S. dollars can consider:

- Spiders (Standard & Poor's Depositary Receipts) index based on the S&P 500 index, based on the 500 biggest companies in the U.S. and a few foreign companies
- Diamonds index based on the Dow Jones Industrial Average

Webs (World Equity Benchmark shares) are traded on the American Stock Exchange (AMEX) and cover the indices for 17 countries.

 Dividends earned on foreign stocks are taxed in Canada as interest income. They do not have the benefit of the dividend tax credit.

CURRENCY RISK

Canadians who buy international investments need to consider the value of the Canadian dollar relative to other currencies, and the impact changes will have on the return of their portfolio. When the Canadian dollar falls, the value of international stocks goes up. But the cost to buy new international investments also goes up.

Suppose you buy 100 stocks of an internationally known American company at US$10 a share when it costs C$1.20 to buy US$1. If the Canadian dollar falls in value to the point where it costs C$1.30 to buy US$1, you have made money on the investment, even if the cost of the shares is still US$10. On the other hand, if the Canadian dollar rises in value to the point where it costs C$1.10 to buy US$1, then you have lost money on the investment, even the cost of the shares in U.S. dollars has not changed.

International equity mutual funds also have a higher risk resulting from currency risk. Even if the fund is purchased in Canadian dollars, the money manager will be buying the investment in the company's local currency. If the value of the Canadian dollar falls in relation to the foreign currency, it will enhance the investment return. If the value of Canadian dollar rises in relation to the foreign currency, it will lessen the return on those foreign investments.

DERIVATIVES

Some international fund managers use investment contracts called **derivatives** to access international markets, rather than buying the stocks directly, where the price of the contract is *derived* from the value of the underlying stock. Some derivative contracts decrease currency exposure and provide increased liquidity and flexibility to the money managers. Other derivative contracts significantly increase the risk to the investor. If in doubt, ask!

In other countries, the government regulation regarding security disclosure may be less stringent than those in North America, adding to the investment risk in some foreign companies and countries. A fund that invests in emerging countries will have more risk, due to policy factors and uncertain economic stability, than an international fund investing in countries with more mature stock markets.

In RRSPs and RRIFs, investors are allowed to hold a percentage of their investments in foreign investments. By maximizing the foreign content to the allowable limit, currently 20 percent, and selecting suitable investments, you can add diversification to your portfolio, which should reduce (but not eliminate) your risk *and* enhance your long-term return.

Purchases, redemptions, switches and the reinvestment of distributions all affect the calculation of your plan's book value.

CHAPTER EIGHT

Tax issues for stock investors

It's not what you make, it's what you get to keep at the end of the day that determines how successful an investor you are.

The good news: transactions made inside an RRSP or RRIF are not taxed in the year they are made. Tax has to be paid when money is withdrawn from these registered plans. Until then, any profits are tax deferred. Remember, however, that all withdrawals are taxed as regular income without any of the advantages for dividend or capital gains. Many Canadians expect their retirement income will be lower than during their working years, and expect that their RRSP contributions will result in a lower lifetime tax bill.

The bad news: for investments held outside a registered plan, investors need to keep track of every transactions they make, including all commissions paid, any interest on borrowed money, as well as their profits or losses. Your monthly or quarterly statement from your broker will summarize all your transactions and provide evidence for tax purposes, even if you do not receive a T5 slip. But the responsibility for the recordkeeping is yours.

TYPES OF INCOME

Canadians can invest to earn three different types of income: interest, dividends and capital gains.

Each type of income is taxed according to different rules. The amount you get to keep depends on these rules (which are found in the Income Tax Act) and your own personal tax rate. Your personal tax bracket is based on the marginal tax rate. A 50 percent marginal tax rate means that for each additional dollar earned, 50 cents is paid to Revenue Canada. A 40 percent marginal tax rate means that for each additional dollar earned, 40 cents is paid to Revenue Canada. If you earn $1,000 in interest income and your marginal tax rate is 50 percent, you will have to pay $500 in income tax.

 Don't let the tax rules determine your investment strategy for you. First, determine the level of risk you are prepared to accept in your portfolio and the appropriate asset mix. Then, and only then, determine the types of investments you will hold and in which account you will hold them.

Interest income is paid to investors who lend money and is earned on savings accounts, Treasury bills, Canada Savings Bonds, GICs, term deposits and bonds. Mutual funds also earn interest income on the short-term money market investments and bonds they hold. Interest income has to be reported each and every year, whether or not it is paid out in cash. For example, Canada Savings Bonds can be purchased on a compound basis. The investor may not actually receive any interest, but the interest earned must still be reported every year.

Dividend income is paid to shareholders on record as a distribution of part of the profits of the corporation. The investor who receives the dividend is the person on record with the transfer agent. Regardless of whether the dividend income was paid out in cash to you or was reinvested in a dividend reinvestment plan, the dividend income is taxable in the year it was received. For individual stocks, unless the dividend was small, you will receive a tax slip for the tax year. Even if you don't receive a tax slip, you still need to report the dividend income on your tax return If it was earned outside your RRSP or RRIF.

Dividends from Canadian corporations receive the benefits of the dividend tax credit, which is designed to encourage investment in Canadian firms by reducing the tax bill on dividend income. The amount of tax due on dividends is calculated by "grossing up" the amount of the dividend income by 25 percent and then applying the dividend tax credit. The result of the calculation is that the tax bill on dividend income is less than the tax bill on interest income.

Dividends earned by foreign companies, including the United States, do not receive the benefit of the Canadian dividend tax credit and are taxed as regular income.

Capital gains are the profits earned on investments and property – in the stock market, on any profits made from selling your shares when they are up in value or when Revenue Canada treats the investment as if it was sold under the deemed disposition rules, such as on death or if you become a non-resident of Canada.

Seventy-five percent of your capital gains are taxable and must be reported on your income tax return. The capital gains is calculated as the proceeds from the sale of the stock or bond less the adjusted cost base of the investment (the price you paid for the investment, including any commission charged). In 1998, 75 percent of the capital gains is taxable on a Canadian resident's tax return. For a profit of $100, the taxable capital gain is $75.

Suppose you invested $2,000 in a stock that is now worth over $12,000. Your tax bill would be calculated as follows:

Proceeds from the sale (after commission)	$12,000
Adjusted cost base	2,000
Capital gain (or profit)	$10,000
Taxable capital gain (75% of $10,000)	$ 7,500
Tax due (assuming a 50% marginal tax rate)	$ 3,750

If Revenue Canada determines you to be an active trader of stocks or bonds, they could consider that you derive your income from your trading and require you to report your capital gains income as regular income – losing the tax-preferred treatment of capital gains income. But most readers of this book shouldn't lose sleep over this slim possibility.

Investors in individual stocks determine when they will pay the tax on their capital gains, depending on when they choose to realize those gains. For example, if you buy a stock at $10 a share, and it does up in value to $25 a share, you can defer paying tax on the $15 gain until you sell. Holders of equity mutual funds often face an annual tax bill when the mutual fund makes a taxable distribution to their unitholders.

A *capital loss* is created when the selling price of an investment is less than the cost of the investment. A capital loss can be deducted from capital gains and can be carried forward until the final tax return. Some investors will review their transactions for the year. If they have a stock in their portfolio that has gone down in value, they may choose to do some tax-loss selling and sell it so that the transaction settles before the end of the year so they can deduct the capital loss from that year's tax return. They can remove losing investments from their portfolio – and be able to use the loss to offset the tax from their capital gains.

FACTOR IN YOUR TRADING COSTS

The investments you buy or sell and when you buy or sell them should not be motivated by the tax rules. That said, if you have an investment you are planning to sell, being able to take advantage of a tax loss is like making lemonade out of lemons.

When you are monitoring the performance of your investments, be sure to include the commission you paid to execute your transactions. Many investors only look at their before-tax returns. However, it is the *after-tax* returns that determine how much of your money you get to keep. The amount of tax you pay on your investments depends on the type of income you earned and the tax bracket you are in.

Investors who receive a substantial portion of their income from income that receives a preferred tax treatment, such as dividends or capital gains income, may be subject to alternative minimum tax (AMT). Alternate minimum tax was designed to ensure that Canadians pay at least a minimum amount of tax on their income, regardless of the tax advantages of certain types of income. (Sorry, there's no way to avoid this.)

 Keep your more aggressive investments outside your RRSP or RRIF, if you have them in your portfolio. Then if they happen to lose money, the capital loss can be used to offset other capital gains. If these investments are held inside a registered plan, there are no tax deductions to help cushion the blow.

CHAPTER NINE

Additional resources

CANADIAN SHAREOWNERS ASSOCIATION

The Canadian Shareowners Association (2 Carlton St., Suite 1371, Toronto, Ont. M5B 1J3) has programs for do-it-yourself investors, including a low-cost investing program focusing on dividend reinvestment.

INTERNET

There are a number of Internet sites where you can obtain stock research and track your investments. Some are free and some charge fees. Some sites you might look at include:

*   the sites of major financial institutions
*   www.canada-stockwatch.com
*   www.sedar.com
*   www.imoney.ca
*   www.bloomberg.com/canada/canada.html

There are also a number of sites that help investors track their mutual fund investments.

INVESTMENT CLUBS

Many Canadians are members of investment clubs, for socializing and profit. The idea is simple. Each member of the club contributes a set amount per month, about $25 or more. At each meeting, the members discuss various corporations and investment ideas. They decide how to invest the money and place their trades through one of the member's brokers or through a discount broker.

By pooling their money, they can learn about specific companies, the market and invest more than they could individually. Besides, if they pick a losing stock, they all have a say in picking it. Likewise, they can all say they helped in the selection if it turns out to be a winning stock!

MARKET SIMULATION GAMES

Readers who are interested in the stock market but are not yet ready to commit with real money might want to check out some of the stock market simulation games on the Internet.

FOR MORE INFORMATION

For more information on how to build your stock portfolio, you may want to:

- read the business, political and economic news in the papers, including *The Globe and Mail*, the *National Post*, *Barron's* and *The Wall Street Journal*, or through the Internet
- read *The Review* published by the Toronto Stock Exchange each month with information on all the stocks listed on the TSE, their P/E ratios, dividend yields, new companies and more
- read the articles in the news relating to personal finance issues, such as retirement, tax and estate planning
- study financial reports for specific companies
- take a course. The Investor Learning Centre and the Canadian Securities Institute of Canada offer courses for the investing public, as well as programs to professionals in the financial industry.

Glossary

ADR American depository receipts are shares of foreign corporations that are held by U.S. banks and trade as stocks on U.S. exchanges

ask the price for which a shareholder is willing to sell a security

benchmark an index used to measure the relative performance of a stock or an asset class

bid the price someone is willing to pay for a security

blue chip a large, mature company with brand-name recognition

board lot a trading unit for securities, usually 100 shares

bull a person who believes stock markets are going to rise

bull market a period in the stock market characterized by rising stock prices

bear a person who believes stock markets are going to fall

bear market a period in the stock market characterized by falling stock prices

capital gain the profit realized when an investor sells an investment; 75 percent of capital gains earned outside a registered plan are taxable

correction a relatively short decline in stock prices when the overall trend is that of a bull market – often creates buying opportunities for astute investors

CIPF Canada Investor Protection Fund provides up to $500,000 if a broker's firm goes under (providing the firm is registered with a major stock exchange in Canada or the IDA)

CUSIP number every security has a unique identification number issued by the Committee on Uniform Security procedures

deflation a period when prices are generally falling

delist when a company is removed from the trading list or the stock exchange for not meeting certain requirements or if the company goes bankrupt

dividend a portion of the corporate earnings paid out to the share-holders on record

fiscal year-end the 12-month period a corporation reports its financial information, which does not have to correspond with the calendar year-end

future a contract for purchase or delivery of an investment at a specific time in the future; most commonly used for commodities, such as oil and gas, gold, and for currencies; they may be used for speculation, or to fix the purchase price

growth investing looking for companies whose earnings are growing faster than the competition; usually an investor is willing to pay a premium price in anticipation of this future income

inflation a period when prices are generally rising, measured by the Consumer Price index (CPI)

institutional investor manages money on behalf of corporations or on behalf of individuals through a mutual fund or a pension fund

interlisted securities companies that are listed on at least one stock exchange

lagging indicator statistics that indicate where the business cycle has been, such as consumer credit levels and the amount businesses spend on capital investments

leading indicator statistics that indicate where the business cycle is heading, such as the unemployment rate and housing starts

liquidity the ability to turn an investment into cash quickly at a reasonable price

long position holding shares of a company in your account

market where buyers and sellers can exchange their goods and services, such as a farmers' market, an antique market or the stock market

non-systematic risk risk that is unique to the stock of a particular company, such as poor management or the demand for its services

odd lot a trade that is not a board lot

preliminary prospectus a document produced in advance of the financial prospectus that contains much of the same information without the final details; designed to see what interest there is in the new issue, but no sales can be made based on this document

price/book ratio the relationship between the share price and the book value of the assets of the company (price to book); value investors look for companies when the value of the shares outstanding totals less than the book value of the company

price/earnings ratio the P/E ratio, or P/E multiple, is calculated as:

$$\frac{\text{current market price per share}}{\text{company's earnings/share for the last 12 months}}$$

The P/E ratio can be useful for comparing one company with other companies in the same industry

prospectus a document that is meant to provide true, plain and full disclosure of all the material facts of the security issue when it is sold initially to the public

share exchange when shares are exchanged for the shares of another class or other company

short selling selling shares you do not own in anticipation of a decline in share prices

stock consolidation the opposite of a stock split

stock market a regulated market where buyers and sellers come together to trade their stocks

stock split a share is exchanged for more shares, such as a two-for-one split when each holder of one share would receive two shares

strategic asset allocation selecting an asset mix between cash, bonds and equities to minimize the downside risk in the portfolio while maximizing the potential return for that level of risk

street name securities that are registered in the name of the dealer, rather than your own

systematic risk the risk of the market itself, such as a bear market

tactical asset allocation selecting an asset mix among cash, bonds and equities given the outlook for the market over the short term; often referred to an market timing

street name a stock registered on your behalf through the brokerage firm

technical analysis the use of charts or other techniques to evaluate a particular company; may include tracking the moving average, the trading volumes or other factors

thinly traded when few investors are willing to buy or sell a particular security; the price from one trade to the next may have larger swings than a stock with more investor interest

trading volume the number of securities that trade in a specific period, often measured daily

value investing looking for companies whose market price is below their book value

**For fifty years, Coles Notes have been helping
students get through high school and university.
New Coles Notes will help get you through the rest of life.**

Look for these NEW COLES NOTES!

BUSINESS
- Effective Business Presentations
- Accounting for Small Business
- Write Effective Business Letters
- Write a Great Résumé
- Do A Great Job Interview
- Start Your Own Small Business
- Get Ahead at Work

GARDENING
- Indoor Gardening
- Perennial Gardening
- Herb Gardening
- Organic Gardening

LIFESTYLE
- Wine
- Bartending
- Public Speaking
- Speed Reading
- Cooking 101
- Cats and Cat Care
- Dog and Dog Care

PARENTING
- Your Child: The First Year
- Your Child: The Terrific Twos
- Your Child: Ages Three and Four
- Raising A Reader
- Helping Your Child in Math

PERSONAL FINANCE
- Basic Investing
- Investing in Stocks
- Investing in Mutual Funds
- Buying and Selling Your Home
- Plan Your Estate
- Develop a Personal Financial Plan

PHRASE BOOKS
- French
- Spanish
- Italian
- German
- Russian
- Japanese
- Greek

SPORTS FOR KIDS
- Basketball for Kids
- Baseball for Kids
- Soccer for Kids
- Hockey for Kids
- Gymnastics for Kids
- Martial Arts for Kids

**Coles Notes and New Coles Notes are available at the following stores:
Chapters • Coles • Smithbooks • World's Biggest Bookstore**

NOTES & UPDATES